Discovery™

I Am a
POLAR
BEAR

Level 2

Written by Lori C. Froeb

Silver Dolphin

D0369888

P1 PRE-LEVEL 1: ASPIRING READERS

1 LEVEL 1: EARLY READERS

2 LEVEL 2: DEVELOPING READERS

- Simple factual texts with mostly familiar themes and content
- Concepts in text are supported by images
- Includes glossary to reinforce reading comprehension
- Repetition of basic sentence structure with variation of placement of subjects, verbs, and adjectives
- Introduction to new phonic structures
- Integration of contractions, possessives, compound sentences, and some three-syllable words
- Mostly easy vocabulary familiar to kindergarteners and first-graders

3 LEVEL 3: ENGAGED READERS

4 LEVEL 4: FLUENT READERS

Silver Dolphin Books
An imprint of Printers Row Publishing Group
A division of Readerlink Distribution Services, LLC
10350 Barnes Canyon Road, Suite 100, San Diego, CA 92121
www.silverdolphinbooks.com

ISBN: 978-1-68412-848-8
Manufactured, printed, and assembled in Guangzhou, China.
First printing, July 2019. GD/07/19
23 22 21 20 19 1 2 3 4 5

Hi there! Welcome to my chilly home.

I am a polar bear and these are my cubs.

We do not see humans very often.

We live far from any cities or towns.

All polar bears live in the Arctic.

The Arctic is the northernmost part of Earth.

Winters are long, dark, and cold in the Arctic.

Summers are short and cool.

Polar bears live in Russia, Norway, Greenland, Canada, and Alaska in the United States.

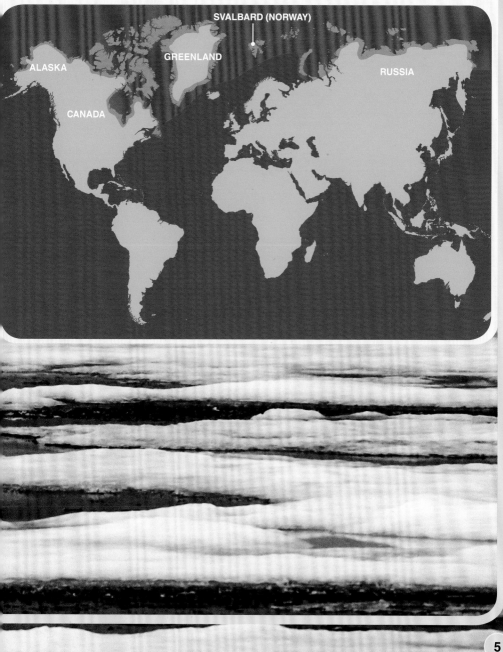

SVALBARD (NORWAY)

GREENLAND

ALASKA

RUSSIA

CANADA

The Arctic is covered by snow and ice for most of the year.

The temperature can drop to minus fifty degrees in winter.

But I am not cold.

Polar bears are covered with very thick fur.

My fur looks white, but each strand is clear.

My fur is very warm and good **camouflage**.

I am hard to spot if I am laying still in the snow.

Under all this fur, my skin is black.

The black color absorbs the sun's light and warms me up!

My body has another way of staying warm: **blubber**!

Blubber is fat. I have a layer of blubber under my skin.

It is four inches thick in places.

The blubber keeps me warm when I swim in the icy water.

Polar bears are great at swimming!

We can swim for days if we need to.

Look at my front paws. They are as big as dinner plates.

I use my front paws like giant paddles in the water.

My paws are great for walking on the snow and ice, too.

The bottoms are covered in tiny bumps.

The bumps grip the slippery ice.

Polar bears are **marine mammals**.

The ocean provides us with food and a place to live.

sea otter

polar bear

dolphin

bearded seal

Dolphins, sea otters, and seals are also marine mammals.

Seals are our favorite food!

Polar bears are the largest **predators** with four legs.

Male bears can weigh as much as ten adult humans.

Females like me are much smaller.

Polar bears spend most of their lives floating on **sea ice**.

Sea ice is frozen ocean water.

I jump from piece to piece to travel.

I also use the ice pieces as resting places when I'm swimming.

I use the sea ice for something else—hunting seals.

Seals come to holes in the ice to breathe.

I can smell a seal's breathing hole from a mile away.

I follow my nose to the hole.

Then I wait quietly and watch the hole.

When a seal pops out of the hole to breathe, I quickly grab it.

My cubs learn how to hunt from watching me.

The sea ice is around from fall to spring.

We eat as many seals as we can.

The seals' blubber makes us fat.

When the sea ice melts in the summer, we move to shore.

There is not much to eat until the ice returns in the fall.

Sometimes a whale **carcass** washes up on the beach.

We eat its blubber and share with other polar bears.

This carcass was a lucky find.

Sometimes a hungry polar bear may hunt a musk ox or reindeer.

Some polar bears will eat seaweed or birds.

None of these things are as good for us as seals.

Many of us eat nothing for months.

We live off our fat until fall.

Earth is warming up and it is taking longer for sea ice to form.

We are spending more time on land.

It is getting harder to find food.

For this reason, polar bears are **vulnerable**.

This means our numbers are getting smaller.

If we do not find a way to survive, we will be **endangered**.

My cubs are strong.

I take good care of them.

I ate a lot of food in the spring before they were born.

I gained more than four hundred pounds!

In the fall, I dug a den in the snow.

I went into the den and rested.

Polar bears don't **hibernate** like other bears.

I did not move much and did not eat for seven months.

Polar bears usually have one, two, or three cubs.

I had two. Twins!

They were born in winter with their eyes closed.

They each weighed less than two pounds.

That is about as much as a small rabbit.

They drank my milk and grew quickly.

In the spring, we left the den.

The cubs learned to walk, swim, and play.

I finally got something to eat.

It had been seven months

Now the cubs watch me hunt on the sea ice.

I smell a seal nearby. It is time for the cubs' lesson.

See you later!

Polar Bear Fact File

Polar bears roll in the snow to clean themselves. Clean fur is warmer than dirty fur.

Polar bears are more likely to be too hot than too cold. A quick swim cools them down.

Almost sixty percent of polar bears live in Canada. That is about sixteen thousand polar bears.

Polar bears are not hunted by any other animals. Humans are polar bears' only predator.

Glossary

blubber: a layer of fat that marine animals use for warmth and energy

camouflage: an animal's coloring that helps it hide and blend in

carcass: a dead body, usually of an animal

endangered: almost none left in the world

hibernate: to go into a deep sleep for the winter. Animals don't eat or drink while hibernating.

marine mammal: mammals that depend on the ocean to live. Whales, polar bears, and sea otters are marine mammals.

predator: an animal that hunts other animals for food

sea ice: frozen ocean water

vulnerable: a species that will become endangered if its habitat keeps shrinking